To the Horizon and Beyond

Student Ministers in Golden Prairie, Saskatchewan, 1929-1975

Edited by Jerome Martin

Published by
Spotted Cow Press • 4216 - 121 Street • Edmonton, Alberta T6J 1Y8

Copyright © 1990
Spotted Cow Press
4216 - 121 Street
Edmonton, Alberta T6J 1Y8

All rights reserved. No part of this publication may be reproduced, stored in a retrieval system, or transmitted in any form or by any means whatsoever without prior permission of the copyright owners.

ISBN 0-9694665-0-1

Edited by:
　Jerome Martin
Graphic Design:
　Melanie Eastley-Harbourne
Page Composition:
　Lu Ziola
Photo Credits:
　Flemming Holm (pages 31, 32)
　Harold King (page 53)
　Jerome Martin (pages 1, 3, 17, 24, 39, 56, 64)

This book is printed on acid-free paper.

Table of Contents

List of Student Ministers 1929-75 v
Acknowledgements vi

Introduction 1
W. Edward Aldworth, 1929 5
E. Clifford Knowles, 1930 8
R. R. W. McGregor, 1938 11
James C. Leadbeater, 1941 16
Donald G. Littlejohns, 1942 19
A. Leonard Griffith, 1944 22
Douglas K. Walker, 1945 23
George D. Watt, 1947 26
Margaret Watt, 1947 29
Flemming Holm, 1948 31
Nettie Wilson (Hoffman), 1949 34
A. L. Evans, 1950-51 40
Violet McCuaig (Crichton), 1952 42

James H. MacIntosh, 1954-55 45
Harold R. King, 1958-59 47
Terry McKague, 1960 55
Franklyn Giffen, 1965 59
Keith Gross, 1966 62
W. Lawrence Harrison, 1969 64
Bill Corkem, 1970 66
Elaine Palmer, 1971 68
Brian N. Walton, 1973 69
Arnold Chamberlain, 1974 70

STUDENT MINISTERS
Golden Prairie United Church
Golden Prairie, Saskatchewan

Year	Name
1929	W. Edward Aldworth
1930	E. Clifford Knowles
1931	A.C. Reynolds
1932	Mr. March (Marsh ?)
1933-34	Ralph Hardwick
1935	James Brooks
1937	Ivan Edwards
1938	R. R. W. McGregor
1939	James Hamilton
1940	J. Keith Woollard
1941	James C. Leadbeater
1942	Donald G. Littlejohns
1943	S. G. Phinney
1944	A. Leonard Griffith
1945	Douglas K. Walker
1946	M. C. Jewell
1947	George D. Watt
1948	Flemming Holm
1949	Nettie Wilson (Hoffman)
1950-51	A. L. Evans
1952	Violet McCuaig (Crichton)
1953	Dirk Blikkendal
1954-55	James H. MacIntosh
1956	Stuart Smith
1957	Allan Beach (Beech?)
1958-59	Harold R. King
1960	Terry McKague
1961	Douglas G. McKenzie
1962	Ross R. Bruleigh
1963	Garry H. Quart
1964	Brian L. Kingsley
1965	Franklyn Giffen
1966	Keith Gross
1967	Rodney Sheets
1968	Robert C. Putman
1969	W. Lawrence Harrison
1970	Bill Corkem
1971	Elaine Palmer
1972	Ken Johnson
1973	Brian N. Walton
1974	Arnold Chamberlain
1975	Bonnie Burnett

ACKNOWLEDGEMENTS

The student ministers and their families who contributed their stories and photographs made this book possible. I thank them for their co-operation and enthusiasm. Special thanks go to Lu Ziola, Melanie Eastley-Harbourne, and Val Smyth who contributed their time and talents to design and produce the book.

My thanks to my wife Merle for her editorial assistance and for contacting the contributors. Thanks also to my parents, Paul and Rose Martin, for their help in planning and producing this book.

Jerome Martin
Edmonton, Alberta
May, 1990

INTRODUCTION

Golden Prairie is a small village located in southwestern Saskatchewan, north of Maple Creek. This area, known as the Palliser Triangle, is one of the driest regions in western Canada. The town was built in the 1920s by German immigrants, many of whom came to Canada via North Dakota.

Golden Prairie

The 1920s were prosperous years for farmers. However, the "dirty thirties" caused many farmers in that area to leave their farms. The period between 1950 and 1980 was prosperous for local farmers, but Golden Prairie – like most small towns and villages in the prairies – decreased in population. In 1959, there were four grocery stores in town; today (1990) there is only one. The lumber yard, the repair shops, and the bulk oil and gas dealerships are gone. Three elevators and the Post Office remain.

The United Church was built in 1927. It was served each summer by "student ministers" who were sent by the Church. These students were either studying theology or considering a career in the ministry. Most of the students who were assigned to Golden Prairie were from the Maritimes or Ontario and had never been "out west."

This book is a compilation of their experiences and impressions, in retrospect. Those of us who shared these experiences remember these students with fondness and respect. Most of them went on to careers in the ministry; several of them stayed in western Canada.

The last student minister assigned to Golden Prairie was Bonnie Burnett, in 1975. Since then the church building has not been used for church services. The one-room manse was sold and moved to a local farm.

This book is my way of saying "Thank You," to the students who lived among us and who brought their joy and talents to small communities like Golden Prairie, and to the people in these communities who gave their love and attention to young people far from home.

The title for this book came from Rev. Donald G. Littlejohns (page 19). "I had never seen such flat land…it stretched to the horizon and seemingly beyond."

Jerome Martin

1 9 2 9

The 1929 summer assignment at Golden Prairie was to be a Home Mission experiment. Dry years had prompted some families to move out; 4 and 6-bushel wheat yields discouraged many. There had been as many as three summer fields in the area concerned. Send someone who would rearrange the pattern: Home Mission Board would advance money for a used car.

Being at St. Andrew's College, I picked up a 1921 Model T coupe, drove by way of Regina and Moose Jaw, dropped Allen Miner with his Supervising Minister at Cadillac, checked in with the Presbytery Home Mission Chairman at Gull Lake and Supervising Minister at Maple Creek, and arrived at Golden Prairie, territory unknown to me, with just 1¢!

Golden Prairie was a new village; the C.P.R. had arrived only in 1928. Everything was new – houses, business places, community hall – and much was still under construction. The first person I met, at his gasoline pump, was Ike Luker, who staked me for a tank of gas. It was on to the Mansell home northwest of Golden Prairie and to the Linacre area where I made arrangements for a room and some meals at the Albrecht home. Johnny and Freida were very accommodating folk.

Plans were made for two sets of services on alternate Sundays – one Sunday trip was about 40 miles, the other about 80. The first was a school northwest of Linacre (was it Peace Valley?), Horsham and Richmound; the second was Surprise school west of Golden Prairie, at the Community Hall when it was completed, and a school in range country to the northeast – all had been appointments for former fields. I would be away from the Albrechts for a couple of days or maybe a week.

Horsham and the range area school proved to be questionable choices. Otherwise, there was encouraging support, both attendance and dollar wise. For those people something like $105 for the Missionary and Maintenance fund was to be commended. At Golden Prairie, Luker initiated conversations about baseball games – when the hour for service was set, there would be no baseball games until after the service. Baseball crowds, uniformed and all, joined in, and the hall was always well filled. Another feature of late Sunday afternoon was Bill Aberhardt's Bible Hour from Calgary.

Midsummer saw a transfer of the Home Mission Superintendent. John Doyle gave way to George Dorey, who visited the students, and whose first visit was to Golden Prairie. He insisted on trying out his new tent and cot, and an overnight storm blew down his tent. Those southwestern Saskatchewan thunder storms were so similar to ones that moved east off Lake Huron they almost made the student homesick.

The Bensteads were no longer young folk. They had come from the Chicago area to a very stoney farmstead in the hills between Golden Prairie and Linacre. She had suffered a broken ankle which had not been properly treated. He needed hernia repairs. They battled stones, unruly horses, rats, and dry seasons. In need of supplies, they would take a few bags of grain by team and wagon to Fox Valley.

Two brothers (was the name Preston?) had come from south of the border and were farming east of Golden Prairie. One day, Roy asked a question he thought an Ontario farm lad should be able to answer. Sow thistle had been advancing westward on the prairie, farmers were apprehensive, and he had weeds he did not recognize: could they be sow thistle? Near his buildings was a patch of healthy-looking Canada thistle.

John Martin's sheep ranch was on the west side of the Big Stick grade southeast from Golden Prairie. Martin and his sheep dogs have been featured at Chicago and New York shows. It was quite a sight: several thousand sheep in the coulee with the ever-alert shepherd and his dogs, and coyotes frequented the area. The Mitchell horse ranch was to the east. That summer arctic explorer Stefansson was on the Maple Creek Chautaqua program, and was entertained at the Mitchell ranch.

Of course, everyone went to the Cypress Hills stampede. Thoughtful folk invited the student to go and he was foolish enough to enter sprint races in which the local Indian lads always took the prizes.

Harry Parsons, postmaster at Richmound, went each week to Medicine Hat wholesale houses for his general store supplies. The student had one of those trips. Driving through the rolling hills of southeast Alberta, there were many miles without sight of current human habitation. Families had already moved out.

At harvest time the student spent several days in Barney Begley's grain truck, where he became acquainted with a grain scoop. It put one on his feet physically, and there were a few dollars for college.

The Home Mission experiment made an interesting summer for the student: not his first pastoral experience. One remembers many conversations: the anxieties, the hopes. It was a very rewarding experience. I did some more growing up and was ready for the second of the six years on the campus.

W. EDWARD ALDWORTH

1 9 3 0

When I arrived in Golden Prairie in 1930 I felt I had a good background to a prairie mission field, having spent the summers of 1925 and 1926 on a field near Biggar. In so far as a warm Saskatchewan welcome was concerned, I was right. There were, however, marked differences. In 1925-26, everything was horse-drawn. In the five hundred square miles I had to cover, I cannot remember a single Model T Ford. In Golden Prairie, anything horse-drawn was also an exception. My horse and buggy in the north was replaced by a 1922 Model T which had stood in the yard of the Superintendent Minister under several inches of snow at temperatures, so I was told, of fifty below. At any rate, it was cold enough to provide me with many problems throughout the summer.

One difference which surprised me was the attitude of at least one family which was critical towards a student who smoked a pipe, played cards, and appeared once or twice in the dance hall. I don't think this affected Church attendance very much, which, despite some wet Sundays, increased steadily until a major tragedy hit the community. This was the death from polio of a 13-year-old boy. So far as I remember, there was no second fatality in the area, though several small children developed colds, high temperatures, etc., which the doctor thought might have been a mild dose. There was, of course, no Salk vaccine at that time and we observed a rather strict quarantine for four weeks of all public meetings. To some extent, this broke the steady growth of Sunday congregations.

Not only was this the first funeral I had to conduct, it was the first funeral I had ever attended. The family concerned and the community were profoundly affected, and so was I. One good soul in Maple Creek sought to reassure me by saying that it had been a "very successful funeral."

In addition to the curtailment of Sunday services, I was very cautious about visiting the homes where there were small children.

Before the polio scare, I had stayed some weeks with Barney Begley, who was then the moving spirit in the building of an 8 x 16 foot shack for the "Preacher." This was on open ground about a quarter of a mile east of the village. Because of very heavy winds we could not nail the long lengths of clapboard, and had to take two days to finish the job. About thirteen men were at the bee, superintended by a carpenter from Maple Creek. I gather from Jim Leadbeater who was at Golden Prairie in 1941 that, by the time the shack had disappeared, a church had been built in the village itself, together with a Manse. So he did not have to transport open pails of water in the Ford, half of which was lost on route!

For a few weeks, we had so-called choir practice. I say "so-called" because they quickly changed to social evenings, very popular and in a way quite in order. But there wasn't much practising.

One of the memories which has stayed with me and has often been used in sermons was the experience of Bill Beach.

Bill had come up from Kansas, I think, in 1905. He arrived in Maple Creek and located with a local attorney. He awoke next morning to find the prairies at Golden Prairie ablaze – set deliberately, it is believed, by the local ranchers who did not welcome the arrival of grain growers who, with their fenced-in crops, would put an end to the open range. Bill had come originally from Pudsey in Yorkshire. As a child, I remember that we said of a man from Pudsey, "Heave a brick at him." I have often used this incident as an illustration of the age-old quarrel between settler and shepherd dating back in history to Cain and Abel. But the Beaches were made of stern stuff and, after living the first winter on frozen potatoes and molasses, lived to build a fine farm and a fine family.

Towards the end of the summer, one of the major concerns of the community was whether members of the Wheat Pool would renew their agreement to join for a further five years. Critics of the co-operative scheme said that as the line elevators were offering 72 cents a bushel and the pools initial payment of 50 cents would not rise above 50 cents, it would be foolish not to accept the line elevators' offer. These are the figures I heard used in argument. After the passage of sixty years, it might be interesting to discover how far I am wrong.

The life and work of the United Church in Golden Prairie was by no means an unqualified success in 1930, but clearly with the building of a church and manse within ten years, there must have been some devoted work by the members of the community to have advanced as well as it evidently did. Long may that devotion and support continue.

CLIFFORD KNOWLES

1 9 3 8

As a theological student at St. Andrew's College, University of Saskatchewan in Saskatoon, in the spring of 1938 I learned that I would spend the summer as student minister near the southwest corner of the province, near Maple Creek. Maple Creek is (now) on the Trans-Canada Highway, on the CNR main line, and about 25 miles from the Alberta boundary. Golden Prairie, where I would live, is about 25 miles to the north and only 18 miles east of Alberta; and Richmound, my other community, is about 20 miles north of that, and only about 10 miles from Alberta.

Golden Prairie sounded like a great place for a summer assignment in the depression year of 1938. Having lived very little farther south than Saskatoon, I looked forward to meeting people and seeing the geography in an area new to me.

It was during the decade of the drought, dust storms, and depression, and it was during Hitler's invasions in Europe, just before World War II. I was in my very early 20s.

With the economy depressed, the church could only fund students "on a shoestring." A decade later summer students could expect to serve a larger territory, but in a car. In the summer of 1938, early in my time at Golden Prairie, I persuaded the Superintendent of Missions, my "boss," probably against his better judgment, to invest $35 in the purchase of a very old Indian motorcycle of World War I vintage.

From the 20-20 vision of hindsight, my congregations would have had better pastoral care if the motorcycle had been vetoed. Time on the machine and time repairing it were somewhat equal. It was old enough to have worn out a carburetor, so it had one from a Model T car; the tires were Model T too: 30" x 3.5". At the end of the summer it was sold again for $30.

Student ministers begin to experience the wonderful privilege, theirs throughout their ministries, of having a ready welcome into most of the homes and hearts of their church families. In each community there are homes in which they are especially welcome, for a meal or even for a bed overnight. As the student comes to know his people he is gradually accepted as a friend and confidant. All the rich variety of human nature and human experience is shared, and can be drawn upon in later years when giving counsel. This was so of Golden Prairie for me.

In the village of Golden Prairie there was a one-room frame house for the student minister. It stood on sloping ground, opposite the school, near the edge of the community. It had windows on three sides, and one door. It was furnished with a bed, chairs, table, kitchen cupboards, and shelves for books, etc.

During the summer, I was visiting one morning at a home in town when the sky darkened increasingly until the lamps had to be lit in midday in order to see at all. It was my first experience of a southern prairie dust storm: the kind that piled up fine sand in fencelines and fields like snow in winter. We stepped momentarily outdoors and, looking up, could occasionally see a glimpse of an instant clear blue, sunlit sky, and then the darkness again. It was Alberta soil, lifted by strong west winds, to settle in the next province. And local soil, too, was being lifted, to be carried farther east.

My hostess and her family had me stay for lunch, and later in the afternoon, when the storm had passed, I walked back to inspect my "manse." It had no foundation, but was supported by cement blocks at the corners. Since the ground sloped down to the west, the supports were taller at that end, and the wind from the west had blown under the house. When I opened the door and looked in, the whole floor was covered with a thick layer of grey sand. But more amazing was that, scattered around the floor, were innumerable perfect, small "craters" of cone-shaped sand, with a circular top and a reverse cone going down to a tiny hole in the floor. The wind blowing under the house had forced the fine grey sand up through holes in the one layer of flooring, forming various sizes of miniature craters.

But a thick layer of sand was on everything in the house. The curtains, drawn gracefully to each side of the windows, were now accented with layers of dust. The bed had been left covered with a colourful patchwork quilt, which was now solid grey with a quarter-inch of sand. Every shelf and every dish in the closed kitchen cupboard was covered with a grey layer of sand. Cleanup required a shovel before there was any use for a duster.

Strange stories could be told of the Southern Saskatchewan dust storms. Some farmers or their families would be on the road to or from their homes when such a storm would catch them. It would be easy to get lost, and it was difficult to see the road or landmarks on the way. I was told that the sand flying through the air and striking barbed-wire fences would generate static electricity, which would then create sparks at the points of the barbs in the fencing. Some persons were able to keep to the road by watching the fences which were outlined by static electricity.

During those Depression days most farmers reverted to horses to save the cash needed for gasoline. Caught on the road in a dust storm, horses could be relied on to find their way home even when the driver was blinded by the storm. Unfortunately, sometimes the horses' eyes suffered inflammation or more serious damage from staying on the job when the human driver could not.

One day I had the opportunity of visiting a large ranch. One of our farmers had a favourite, very old horse which had been retired to pasture. But something about the horse's health required that it be put to death, and the farmer didn't have the heart to do it. But he had a friend who was a rancher, south of Maple Creek, who would do the job. He invited me to come along, partly, I think, to occupy his mind on the trip home after saying farewell to his faithful horse. So we drove about 40 miles south with his truck, while he told me about the days before farmers settled on that part of the prairie, when there were no fences permitted. Cattle and horse ranchers were the first settlers, and they let their animals roam freely at all seasons, living off the natural grass, or "prairie wool." They would paw through the snow to reach the grass, and come through the bitter winter with thick coats and hardy muscle. In spring the ranchers would join in a round-up to brand calves with the brand of their mothers. Railway carloads of cattle or horses would be shipped out from time to time. When farmers began to arrive to homestead and fence their land, there was a period of "wild west" crisis and sometimes violence, but that was now in the past.

Now we were on our way to a real western ranch, south of Maple Creek, in the famous Cypress Hills. The area has a unique history, geography and wildlife of its own. Its highest point is 3,000 feet above sea level, and higher than Banff, Alberta.

Eventually, we came to a ranch gate, a wide-open gate, but one that no horse or cow will go through, because they are afraid to walk on the series of parallel pipes which do not offer a solid, flat footing, but which allow a car or truck to drive straight over. But it was miles farther, along dirt tracks in the grass, before we came to the ranch buildings on the rising slope of the Cypress Hills. The old horse was left in a corral, and we entered the wide-spreading , old home for the noon meal. The ranch was so large and the buildings so isolated, that it was out of the question to send the children to the nearest school, so there was a live-in teacher for the several children of the family. After the meal and a short visit, my driver gave his aged horse a final, loving pat and went sadly to his truck. On the drive home we made sure to avoid silence and to keep the conversation going.

There are scattered visual memories:
- of church services conducted in school rooms with adults, as well as children, crowding into children's desks
- of visits to homes to get acquainted with family after family
- of the stir in the small community every second Wednesday when a short mixed train chugged up the spur railway tracks, and then returned
- of a young man who lived with his mother in Richmound, who was sensitive about his remarkable height of over 7 feet. Cars were taller then than now, but when this man stood beside one, it looked very small. He was so accustomed to stooping to enter doors that he

was said to have instinctively stooped while walking up the slope into a grain elevator beside the railway. (The doors were large enough to admit a loaded hayrack.) I was told that just once he had exploited his height to entertain. At that time it was not yet recognized as racist to stage "black-faced comedy," and this young man appeared on stage with several others, playing a banjo and singing. For him to sit cross-legged as he played and then to lift the top leg and cross legs the other way, was very amusing, and won him considerable applause.

Another commentary on the way times have changed was an incident in a church service in Richmound. One Sunday three young girls showed up in the congregation, possibly to size up the young minister, and possibly on a mutual "dare." They were known by my congregation to be from Roman Catholic homes, and I would think it took a lot of courage in that small community, where everyone was known, to turn up for worship, especially across the deep gulf in that era between Catholics and Protestants. Roman Catholics were being warned not even to attend Protestant weddings. These girls were a little self-conscious and a bit "giggly." They would not touch the hymn books, as if they had been forbidden to participate in any way. The contrast with today's fraternization between the "separated brethren" of Protestant and Catholic clergy shows how far we have already come since then.

Raw recruits as we were, we summer students ought to salute the tolerance and fortitude, the friendship, and sometimes the guidance, of our summer hosts and hostesses. To have Christian leadership for only one-third of the year, and then only from those learning to be leaders, says something about the generous spirit of those we tried to serve.

R. R. W. McGregor

1 9 4 1

It was a long train ride from Halifax, Nova Scotia, to the Canadian West and darkness had fallen over the Prairies as the train arrived in the town of Maple Creek, Saskatchewan. I knew little of the West, having grown up on the Atlantic coast in Nova Scotia. The great stretches of open country fascinated me and I wondered what it would be like living on the Prairie for the next few months. Golden Prairie was my destination.

I found it on the map, but that told me little about it except that it was a considerable distance from the railroad. It was getting late in the evening; would there be someone there to meet me and drive me to Golden Prairie? If not, what would I do? I had little money to look after my needs until I could reach Golden Prairie. The train stopped at the station as the conductor called out, "Maple Creek." I left the train and stood on the platform as the train moved on. Then a man came up beside me and said quietly, "Are you the student for Golden Prairie?" Oh, so quickly, I said, "Yes!" and felt like hugging Barney Begley and his wife. They took me the 30 miles north to what would be my home town for the next few months, and stopping outside a Church, Mr. Begley said, "Here's the Church," and then pointing to a neat little one-room building alongside, he said, "And there's the Manse."

That was the beginning of a wonderful summer. However, I still remember my sense of shock when I realized I was to live there in the Manse and look after myself, except that each evening I would be entertained for dinner at the home of some member of the Congregation. That was a real comfort, for I knew little about meal preparations and even

The manse

breakfast and lunch looked like quite a problem. But I learned quickly and soon began to enjoy my culinary tasks.

It does not take long to become acquainted in a small community and especially in the Canadian West. There, hospitality is an accepted way of life, and soon I felt at home in the town and with the people of Golden Prairie. The Church was a new building, beautifully cared for, and it spoke eloquently of the deep commitment of the members of this congregation. I soon became aware that the focal point of the commitment was at the Sept General Store, where Mr. and Mrs. Sept and family showed, by example and loyalty, that the Church was a significant influence in their own lives and in the life of their community. The Congregation was not large in numbers, but the families involved were all very loyal and attendance at the services remained fairly constant throughout the summer. The organist and choir leader was Evelyn Sept and with her music she added a great deal to every service.

The other preaching appointment on the charge was Richmound, which was, if I remember correctly, about 20 miles north. The services there were at 2:30 pm Sunday afternoons. Unfortunately, the Church was situated quite close to the ball field, and as there were ball games most Sunday afternoons, we soon found it necessary to begin our services earlier in order to finish before the games would begin. So, preacher, beware of long sermons! When the Church service was ended, most of the congregation moved over to the ball field and took their preacher with them. (Some good games!)

Since my mode of travel on the charge was by bicycle, I would prevail upon some kind person to drive me to Richmound following the morning 11 am service at Golden Prairie. When I remained in Richmound to do some visiting during the early days of the week, I would catch a drive with someone going south later in the week and thus return to my home base.

It was a wonderful summer for me and, when I left in late September to return to University, it was with a new appreciation of the Canadian West, of the hospitality of its people, and with wonderful memories of many new friends on the charge – the Septs, the Begleys, the MacLarens, the Ketchums, and so many others, whom I recall in memory from time to time. My one regret is that I have never had the opportunity to return to the charge to tell the people there what a support they were to me.

I feel my appointment to the Golden Prairie pastoral charge was one of the early blessings bestowed upon me by the United Church.

JIM LEADBEATER

1 9 4 2

I believe it must have been around mid-May, 1942, when I arrived in Golden Prairie, immediately after the spring term. I wanted to go west because I had never had the opportunity to travel beyond the Maritime provinces. Another reason was that I grew up on Saturday matinees when we lived for seven years in Saint John, N.B. The feature movie was usually a cowboy movie, so that our favourite game was cowboys and Indians. Our heroes were Tom Mix, Roy Rogers, the Lone Ranger – daredevils like that. Added to that was the enthusiastic report of Jim Leadbeater who enjoyed his summer in Golden Prairie the previous year. Nowhere else in Canada could you find a name like Golden Prairie except out on the western plains and that is where I asked to be placed.

I found the trip by train from Halifax seemingly endless. First, the procession of trees on both sides of the train for hours on end in New Brunswick and the same thing again only with added rocks north of the lakes in Ontario. I had never seen such flat land as I saw in Manitoba. It stretched to the horizon and seemingly beyond. Beyond that, I started to miss the trees. I could hardly see any. The land seemed so vast and empty. I thought it must be a lonely place to live. Another impression I received was that the people on the train were more friendly than I was used to. While in the Maritimes, it was not common to seek out strangers for conversation, it seemed to be the custom on the prairies. Perhaps it was easy for them to spot an

Easterner, for before long, I had several people around me expressing an interest in who I was, where I had come from, and where I was going. They found it hard to believe that I had never seen a real live cowboy, except in the movies. One said he would introduce me to one on the train and sure enough he brought me to a fellow, not much older than myself, who said he was a rodeo cowboy. He even gave me a picture of himself in his rodeo outfit and autographed it. No doubt he was well known in the west, but to me it was just another name. I have long since lost the photo, but I have never forgotten the feeling of being included in their interest and made to feel welcome by people I had never seen before or would likely see again.

        The overwhelming discovery for me was the warmth and degree of friendship that awaited me at Maple Creek where I was met at the station, continued in the car to Golden Prairie and was an ever-present reality throughout my stay there. I was impressed by the strong community feeling that was there. The people cared very much for their little town and made it an attractive place to live in spite of the shortage of water and such problems as dust storms and grasshoppers. The United Church was a pretty little church, well cared for both inside and out, and located right on the main street. Services were held every Sunday morning and at Richmound in the afternoon where Western hospitality was equally evident.

        Faced with the prospect of preparing a lot of meals for myself, which I never learned to do, I went to Sept's store and asked the attractive clerk what she would recommend for a ready-made breakfast cereal. I came out with a big bushel bag of puffed wheat. The supply outlasted me. I ate all I could eat, gave it to any guests who would come into the cozy little manse, fed it repeatedly to the members of my Trail Ranger Group, but in the end "my boys" found enough to fill the kettle and every other pot or pan they could locate in the kitchen cupboards. I surrendered. The puffed wheat got the better of me. I don't remember eating puffed wheat again after that.

        I encountered one of those strange coincidences in Golden Prairie. One day while enjoying a car drive with friends, we passed by Surprise School. Later I learned that my mother taught in that school for a year after the First World War, travelling all the way from

Charlottetown, Prince Edward Island, at the request of her uncle, a Mr. Matthews, who had a farm at Surprise.

Well, the west got in my blood and I knew I wanted to have my ministry here. In November of 1943 I married Evelyn Sept and we have served the United Church for 39 years, until retirement, in Alberta. We have three children and five grandchildren. So, Golden Prairie, which was so good to us, has a very special place in our memories.

DONALD G. LITTLEJOHNS

1 9 4 4

Now in retirement I have difficulty recalling details of that very brief chapter which took place before I was ordained. I do remember that it was my first and only experience of Western Canada and my first of life in a small community.

A. Leonard Griffith

I had completely lost touch with Golden Prairie until last year when I was preaching in Zion Church, Moose Jaw, where a former teacher in the Golden Prairie school gave me a photograph. She roomed at the home of Peter and Katie Langlands where I took my meals. The picture shows me standing by the 1928 Chevrolet car which the church folk bought for my transportation.

I have some happy memories of Golden Prairie, others which are not so happy. Had I been more mature at the time I should have been less unreasonable in my expectations and more grateful for the measure of response to my ministry. In fact, I have often wished for the opportunity to go back and do it over again.

A. LEONARD GRIFFITH

1945

Having been born and raised in Saskatchewan, I did not find Golden Prairie unusual when I arrived in late April, 1945, to spend the summer as the United Church student minister. It may have been a little smaller than some of the places where I had lived and where my father, Earle H. Walker, had ministered (Salvador, Maryfield, Sintaluta, Carievale, Drinkwater), but it certainly was no smaller than the other places I had served as student minister (Waldeck/Rush Lake in 1941-42; Peebles/Windthorst in 1943-44). Even the severe dust storm early in my stay at Golden Prairie was reminiscent of the years I lived at Carievale (1931-37). So much dust seeped through the single-ply walls of the neat little manse next to the church that the keys of my portable typewriter wouldn't move afterward and the outline of my head showed on the pillow on which I had slept.

The Second World War came to an end while I ministered at Golden Prairie. Church headquarters had anticipated the cessation of hostilities in the European theatre and had provided a service of thanksgiving to be used when the time came. A service was held in the Golden Prairie church and the order of worship provided was followed. No such service was held when the war in the Asian theatre suddenly ended later that summer after atomic bombs had been dropped on Hiroshima and Nagasaki. The fact that we had entered a new era, the atomic age, didn't register with me at the time.

An automobile, a 1928 Chevrolet, was provided for the student minister at Golden Prairie. I had used a bicycle to get around in the previous four summers so this was a vast improvement. However, there were a couple of disadvantages. It was still war time and tires were rationed. A blowout threatened to put the car out of commission, but Ed Sept (the Septs were enormously supportive of student ministers and wonderfully kind) somehow produced a tire and kept the Chev on the road. The other problem was that the make of car had a vacuum gas feed which could be disrupted by a grain of sand or a hair. This sometimes necessitated syphoning gas out of the main tank and transferring it to the small feeder tank above the engine – a wretched business. The Wilde brothers at Richmound (part of the charge) regularly worked on this problem, but without lasting success.

Maple Creek presbytery inaugurated a summer camp at Cypress Hills Park in 1945. I was part of a work crew that undertook to prepare the site for use. We had to clear ground and pitch tents, make a trail to the water supply, and prepare the most primitive kind of toilet facility (a plank between two trees with a pit underneath). A lapse of good judgement scheduled a girls' camp to pioneer the site and when the leaders arrived a day early and looked at what we had prepared, they sat down and wept (with our full understanding and sympathy). I took a carload of boys from Golden Prairie and Richmound to the camp later. We had a good time, but they may still remember being ill after taking turns syphoning gas to keep the church Chev's wonderful vacuum system working – or rather, compensating for the non-functioning of the system.

The manse through a Church window

One notable thing I did in the summer of 1945 was to start giving regular Sunday evening worship services at the Bitter Lake German Congregationalist Church about 10 miles west of Golden Prairie. I had met a young man out that way who said that he didn't attend the church of his parents because the services were in German and he (and others of his generation) were not fluent enough in that language to be able to participate. So I volunteered to conduct services and there was a good response during the three months I did this. I have often wondered if subsequent student ministers continued to go to Bitter Lake.

    I stayed in Golden Prairie a few days longer than was my intention. A major snow storm in the latter part of September closed the road to Maple Creek for several days. Don Littlejohns (who had been student minister at Golden Prairie in 1942 and who had married Evelyn Sept) was also delayed by the storm so we had the opportunity to get well acquainted before we eventually got away on the weekly train to Medicine Hat and thence eastward (Don to the Maritimes; me to my parents' home in Moose Jaw and then on to Saskatoon for my final year at St. Andrew's College). In 1952, both Don and I began 16-year ministries in Calgary – Don at St. Paul's and I at St. Matthew's.

    My wife and I detoured to Golden Prairie and Richmound on our way to Saskatoon in 1988 and were saddened to find the church boarded up and the little manse gone.

DOUGLAS K. WALKER

1 9 4 7

The summer of 1947 was a challenging and exciting time for us at Golden Prairie, Richmound and Bitter Lake.

On the 2250-mile trip from Toronto to Golden Prairie in our 1932 Chevrolet, we tried to visualize what the future might be like, different as it would be from the previous summer in northern Saskatchewan at Shell Lake.

Though the terrain and the environment turned out to be vastly different, we soon found out that the church folk there were also warm, friendly, and supportive in so many ways. It did not take long to feel at home as together we shared in our Lord's work, and took our place in community activities.

Margaret and I had been married in 1945 while I was in the RCAF, and we had the privilege of being together on both summer fields, a type of "two for the price of one" (almost) situation! The church at large, the pastoral charge, the community, and the two of us all benefitted from the "innovative" arrangement.

From the first Sunday to the last one on September 15th, we appreciated and enjoyed the loyalty at worship and the Christian fellowship we experienced in worship, meetings, visiting with the families, midweek groups for young and old, as well as sharing in times of joy and sadness.

Unfortunately, Margaret had to have her appendix out at Maple Creek hospital on May 28th. It was an unexpected set-back, but she recuperated well. The folk on the charge were most kind and helpful and the Health Unit was exceedingly generous in including her in their coverage!

Morning Sunday School and church services were held at Golden Prairie. Richmound held their Sunday School and worship early Sunday afternoon. When the Good Hope Church at Bitter Lake was added not long after we arrived, that service was in the evening. In between Sunday services, and when visiting, we would be invited to have a meal with families in the congregations, and get to know them better.

Margaret and I shared in the Sunday Schools, Vacation school, junior and two senior young people's groups, the summer camp at Cypress Hills, the communicant classes, and the women's groups. Such times were highlights for us. I will never forget the trip taken with the boys to Vodaham's dam. We set out July 11th, on a Friday, afternoon, with about eight boys, and camping equipment for overnight, including wood from railway ties (to build a fire), replacing the back seat in our old car. On the way we took a short cut through a supposedly dry grass slough only to see too late that it wasn't dry! Two hours later, with help from Mr. Jex and his tractor, we headed for our camping spot, supper, games, and a sleep under the stars.

Nor will we forget the Young People's outing to explore the haunted house on the main road, or the unique experience of being the first English-speaking student minister for the German-speaking congregation of Good Hope church, and trying to lead the congregation in English hymns without a choir, or pianist. Nor surprisingly, the next Sunday, they had the piano repaired and had secured a pianist!

Then there was the time during the evening service at Good Hope when the centre light ran out of gas and quit during the singing of Work for the Night is Coming. It was removed, filled, lighted and brought back in to be hung again on the hook on the ceiling during my sermon. The congregation, eyes on the light, swayed back and forth with the attempts of the man on the chair in the middle of the aisle, trying to locate the ceiling hook. Finally, while I continued with the sermon, a loud male voice sounded, "A little to the left," and the lamp was hung, the congregation relaxed, and I finished the sermon. They were a fine faithful folk, as were those at the other two points on the charge.

At various times, I also had an evening service at Maple Creek United Church, returning Mondays after staying overnight at one of the homes there.

The summer was a real training experience filled with the joy of working together with such supportive, kind, gracious, and patient folk of strong and deep faith and good humour. I trust that the people, young and old, grew in faith, in Christian service, and in deeper commitment to our Lord, even as they helped us to do, as we were co-workers together in the summer of 1947.

GEORGE D. WATT

1947

We arrived in Golden Prairie May 2, 1947, in the evening. It had been a windy, dusty day ever since we left Moose Jaw early that morning. We had spent the week driving out from Toronto in our 1932 Chevrolet. We wondered what we would find when we got to Golden Prairie. I was having visions of a tumbledown "manse-shack"

The actual sight was much more pleasant. The church was a nice stucco building, the manse, a neat little house, painted white. The women next door sent us to see Mrs. Colby, who showed us into the manse, then showed her kindness and sensitivity by leaving us alone. We were to find that Mrs. Colby proved to be a thoughtful, supportive friend throughout the summer. The women of the congregation had made sure that the manse was spotlessly clean, a curtain was hung across the middle to divide the house into two rooms, and thus create a bedroom, and the cupboard was stocked with food. It was wonderful to be made to feel so welcome. We felt that we had reached an oasis in the desert!

After unpacking our suitcases and George's trunkful of books, we washed off most of the dust and grime, fell into bed and had a wonderful undisturbed sleep.

The next day George Murray, the church secretary, paid us a visit. He was a kindly man, a widower bringing up several sons and a little daughter, Margaret Rose, on a farm near town. After welcoming us, he said, "The congregation didn't relish a student minister bringing a wife. They have never had a married student, and it meant adding $1.00 per week to the student's food allowance (from $4 to $5), but I said that she would make up for the extra cost, so I hope you won't let me down!"

On Sunday, the congregation was enthusiastic and friendly, and there was a good choir. George Murray went with George to Richmound, to show him the way.

May went by very quickly, filled with meetings, Sunday School, church services, young people's groups, and many visitors to the manse. Unfortunately for me, I developed appendicitis, and had an operation in the Maple Creek hospital May 28th, then went home to Brandon, Manitoba, to recuperate for a month. I returned in July when George was helping at the Cypress Hills camp, enjoyed two days there and came back with him to Golden Prairie. Everyone was very kind and friendly, and welcomed me back with visits and gifts of food.

I remember helping with a Vacation School in August. My group of girls made rag dolls. George's group of boys made birdhouses. We learned songs and hymns and games too, and some of the young women in the congregation were most helpful with all the activities. The children were great fun and I am sure I learned more from them than I taught them.

We planted a garden, but watched it burn, shrivel and finally blow away. Ever since then I have had a great deal of sympathy for all prairie farm families!

I marvel at the patience and long-suffering and kindness of congregations who have summer students year after year, "train them up in the way they should go," and send them back to University and ordination. We learned a great deal from our "summer placements," and think of them with warm gratitude.

MARGARET WATT

1 9 4 8

I don't know that I did anything of much significance while at Golden Prairie. To paraphrase St. Paul, one sows, another waters, and someone, somewhere, perhaps only many years later, reaps a harvest. The ministry is like that. Nellie McClung had a book entitled Sowing Seeds in Danny. Who knows what seeds they are that have borne fruit.

I started my first Cub Pack that summer. I had taken a course in scouting during the winter, and here was my chance to practise what I had learned. There were twelve boys, some of them only eight. The Principal of the school at the time (Rudyard Henderson) had quite a large family, including a son who had just completed Grade 10. He helped me with the boys and took over in the fall. He was too young to be officially a Cubmaster, but we manufactured some fiction that permitted him to carry on. The Pack was still in operation the following spring

The Golden Prairie Cub Pack

Murray Krahn at the Manse, 1948.

when the new student arrived. There was just one elder (George Murray) in the congregation at the time. He was kind enough to write and tell me about the Cub Pack. I also tried to start a Scout Troop but that fell through when my assistant moved away.

Of the Cubs, I remember just one name: Marvin Colby. He lived just across the street with his parents and two older sisters, Lorraine and Frances. I said to him one day, "Marvin, you have a wonderful mother." His face lit up and he agreed enthusiastically. Mrs. Colby and Lorraine taught Sunday School.

Having grown up on small farms in Nova Scotia I suppose I adjusted more easily to conditions on student fields than did most students. But, oh, it was hard work pedalling that old bike across the prairie with the wind against me. It was my first summer on the prairie. I had spent one summer in the park belt, in the Turtle Lake country, but this was my first summer in the southern part of the province. How dry it was, for a while. It hadn't rained for weeks – and then it started. Softly at first, then gathering force. I stood in the doorway of the manse, watching it. Then I became aware that every doorway on the street was similarly occupied. We drank in that blessed rain. It meant so much in a parched land. I thought of the hymn:

> "The dawn of God's dear Sabbath
> breaks o'er the world again
> like some sweet summer morning
> after a night of rain.
> It comes as cooling showers
> on some exhausted land,
> like shade of clustered palm trees
> on weary wastes of sand."

I loved the children, and the little boys particularly used to visit me. I taught some of them to play chess. One little fellow came to see me on my last day there, while I was packing, and I took his picture. That same day one of the mothers brought me a roast chicken to eat on the long journey home. The people on the student fields were a kind, patient lot, who probably taught us a great deal more than we could ever teach them. I sat at the table in so many houses (and washed and dried dishes in almost as many). Many of the women, when baking, made up a little parcel of goodies and sent it over to me by one of the children; perhaps more so at Golden Prairie than anywhere else I have been.

As I look at the pictures I am impressed by the condition of the church property. Loving hands had cared for it and made sure it was painted and neat when many people had little money to spend on their properties.

I also held services at Richmound. Some of my predecessors had served a German community some miles to the west, but for some reason I never held a service – I think transportation was a problem. It would have been interesting to have carried on a program in that community, since I understood a little German, but it never materialized.

I took a week off during the summer and attended a youth camp in the Cypress Hills, not as a leader, just for a change. I learned to swim that week. I had grown up within walking distance of Northumberland Strait with its lovely beaches, and gone out in fishing boats, but had to go to Saskatchewan to learn to swim. When I arrived at the Camp I realized how much I missed the Nova Scotia forests. I felt at home there, splitting firewood for the camp. But, oh, how cold it was at night.

One leaves behind a bit of oneself in each place where one has lived, and takes along a part of the place and the people. I have an impression that by the time I arrived at Golden Prairie (my fourth student field) a longer stay might have been in order. Certainly, the system was a poor one, and we students should have spent some time in close association with older ministers rather than always being sent out to sink or swim on our own.

FLEMMING HOLM

1 9 4 9

Golden Prairie – to me – was not so much a place as an education. It was a five month learning experience somewhat like Clinical Pastoral Education is today, the difference being that I was the student and also the student's supervisor.

The name, Golden Prairie, seemed to me somewhat idyllic, conjuring up images of fields – both material and spiritual – "ripe unto the harvest." In actuality, the yield was relatively disappointing. In Golden Prairie, I realized the meaning of "dust storm" during which time it was impossible to see across the street. One sensed the eeriness of isolation while watching the amazing build-up of sand on the ledges as it filtered through the framework around the closed windows. There too I was introduced to grasshoppers; a credulous Easterner suddenly became aware of the ravages wrought by their well-organized army. That summer the harvest went down the drain and it appeared to me that my labours as a student minister were also doomed to failure. (I was very impressed, however, with the indomitable spirit of the Saskatchewan farmers and quite possibly they inspired me to have hope for the future.)

I arrived on a Saturday afternoon in April and, the larder being empty in my little one-roomed manse, I was very appreciative of an invitation out to supper. My kindly hostess put me at ease with her and the family until part way through the meal at which time her husband came home "under the influence." As soon as he discovered that I was the student minister, he proceeded to pick a fight with me and, strangely enough, I bade a hasty retreat after helping with the dishes.

That was only the beginning. The next day I conducted my first service in the attractive, stucco church next door to the manse. As might be expected, we had a "full house" with all the believers, semi-believers and non-believers, prompted by curiosity if not by the desire to worship. (We even had a full choir and not all churches can boast one of those.) At the conclusion of the service, after all of us had stood around in the sunshine together, one pillar of the church remained to enlighten me. "Did you see the man who helped me take up the offering? That's Mr.___. He works part-time in the liquor store. Do you remember the tall lady in the choir behind you? She's Mrs.___. She's applied for a license to run a beer parlour here in town and we're going to have a vote two weeks tomorrow. I hope you're going to speak out against it because there's no one else to do it." A strange malaise took possession of me ... such was my introduction to life in Golden Prairie.

During the next two weeks, with so little time to establish new friendships, a dark cloud of dread hovered over me. I recalled stories of my father and my uncle who – during World War I – never once had accepted their daily rum ration even when they were fighting at the front in France. I remembered my formerly-Methodist mother describing her father's conversion at which time he discarded both the bottle and the weed. I thought of moving stories I had read of a fairly new group called Alcoholics Anonymous. I discovered that most of my new neighbors came from European backgrounds where beer and more potent beverages were a part of the culture. It seemed, in my brief survey, that there were only one or two abstainers in my congregation apart from me and, of course, I did not have a vote. What to do? Should I follow my conscience, in which case I would probably estrange my "flock" even before we got to know each other, or should I say "Que sera, sera" (Whatever will be, will be), recognizing that I could not possibly sway the outcome if I tried? Meanwhile, I received unsolicited materials from the Temperance Society in Saskatoon and became painfully aware that "I, even I only, Lord, am left" to speak out on this issue. Yet the calendar told me that, having estranged my congregation by endorsing abstinence, I would have to endure yet nineteen Sundays in what promised to be a hostile atmosphere. "Woe is me, Lord, for I am undone."

A new thought came to me. What if Mrs.___ chanced to be sick just that one

Sunday? With a twenty-four hour flu, she could be spared any embarrassment and also make it easier for me. Well, as with all unworthy prayers, this one was not answered. That memorable morning I stood behind the curtains in my one-roomed manse and saw Mrs.___ en route to church. The hour was at hand.

The service proceeded smoothly until the announcements, at which time I mentioned – in as natural tones as possible – a vote about to take place in our community where we, as Christians, need act responsibly. Citing but one statistic about alcohol, I suggested that we ask ourselves what Jesus Christ might do in this situation and act accordingly. My sermon was on "Christian Love" with no references to the following day, but as of the time I had mentioned the word "vote," I seemed to feel invisible darts from the choir loft. Following the benediction, I stood outside the door to greet my parishioners. Mrs.___ shot past me as if she had taken a laxative and could think of only one thing. Immediately thereafter came her constant, woman friend, exclaiming in a doleful tone, "You'll be sorry you ever mentioned that!" and I realized she was not referring to Christian Love. The handwriting was on the wall.

Returning from the afternoon service at Richmound, I was feeling very despondent. I picked up Weymouth's translation of the New Testament and started to read Paul's letter to young Timothy. In short order I came across the words, "Thou, therefore, endure hardness as a good soldier of Jesus Christ." I became aware that that advice was for the young missionary of the first century, but it was also for the Emmanuel College student at Golden Prairie in the summer of '49. It helped.

Alcohol was indeed a problem in our area, disruptive of many lives, but there was more to Golden Prairie than that. I could write of numerous memorable visits that summer: with the elderly woman who let the love of God shine through despite her not too supportive husband; with a young mother who, in ignorance, was giving aspirins to her two-year old as if they were candy; with a couple where the wife was bedridden, yet her disabled husband tried to care both for her and the fields; of the farmhouse where I arrived on my bike to be greeted by a dog who sprang out of nowhere and sunk his teeth into my thigh; of Rose and Paul Martin and their three "kids" whom I came to know and cherish increasingly as the summer wore on.

I also had visitors, and with the little manse being directly across the street from the pool hall, the people of Golden Prairie were my chaperones. On my first Sunday in town I was advised of a man, a middle-aged bachelor in my church, who had written the Home Missions Superintendent in Regina to protest having a woman minister. A "she" was preposterous! On my third Sunday, late afternoon, the gentleman was at my door, inviting me to go for a car-ride. He obviously had changed his mind about "she's." That warmed my heart even though I had not accepted his invitation. As the summer progressed, another parishioner tried to sell me on romantic love, determined not to take "no" for an answer. Was I ever thankful that the kitchen table was so big! It was my sole line of defense. I thought of making a run for the door but realized that – in no time flat – the latest "scoop" would be all over town; my only alternative was to keep the table between us, no matter how many times he changed direction. It was like a game of tag and he was "it" but, thank goodness, "it" was finally exhausted.

Vacation school was a pleasant interlude with Bible stories, music, crafts and games. Even more memorable was the CGIT Camp in Cypress Hills. I, the director, felt slightly "wet behind the ears," having schoolteacher-leaders there who were decidedly more mature and experienced, but youth called to youth – as did those beautiful Hills to this Easterner.

For several years, I had wondered what I would be like when conducting a funeral. Ever since I had attended a Pentecostal funeral service in Ottawa where I sensed the congregation's malaise when the Minister stopped to weep, I had told myself that I must never become emotional like that in public. For the sake of the mourners I must keep my feelings in check. But would my emotional poise prove adequate when confronted by others' tears? The summer of '49 helped me in this regard when I conducted my first funeral in Richmound. Fortunately, it was not characterized by pathos. In fact, the schoolhouse was not big enough and so we had to use the community hall as our "chapel." A dance had been held there the previous night and, unfortunately, it had been raining. Consequently, we not only had to remove inappropriate posters from the wall, but we also had to use shovels to get rid of the gumbo on the floor. A woman kindly volunteered to play the hymns, but had I known how slowly she handled the piano keys (two notes of the melody to one good breath), we would have dispensed with the music. The deceased was an elderly bachelor with no relatives, and I discovered that most of his Lutheran neighbors did not join in the singing. Thus, I felt compelled to sing very lustily to compensate for a non-existent choir and a non-participating congregation. (Can you imagine being the soloist without a solo voice?) I finally pronounced the benediction at which point our volunteer funeral director took over. The casket was a rough, non-pretentious one, hand-made for the occasion. The "hearse" was a large, bright red truck, never before used in this capacity. The lead vehicle in the cortege was a small pick-up truck, driven by the kindly man from the local telephone office and carrying the young woman minister who had no knowledge of the cemetery's location. We proceeded at a dignified rate, temporarily discussing things other than funerals, until the driver exclaimed, "Oh my gosh! I should have turned at that last corner!" So it was that we led the funeral procession several miles out of its way. Finally, the brief committal service was accomplished, but then, to my amazement, everyone lingered to watch the grave filled in because there had been rumours of stealing from corpses. I have conducted hundreds of funerals since that day but I am ever so grateful that my first one was not painful – in the sense of sorrowful – and that up until the present, God has made me strong even amidst tragic circumstances, thereby enabling me to help those most in need.

      I returned to Golden Prairie in the summer of '78, unprepared for the fact that it had become a ghost town. So many buildings had completely disappeared! The nice, little United Church was still there but a big tree, fallen across the front steps, symbolically and literally barred our entrance. Going in via the basement, I experienced a blend of emotions up in the sanctuary. One could not help but feel nostalgic! Thinking of former worshippers who have entered into the Life Beyond, I felt as though I should sing, "For all the saints who from their labours rest." Yet, mindful of those who have become active in the Church elsewhere, it seemed more appropriate to choose "Now thank we all our God."

Interior of Golden Prairie Church

    Church buildings, like our physical bodies, serve a worthy purpose but there comes a time when both must be abandoned. We have the glorious assurance, meanwhile, that God's Spirit is not curtailed and that the "church is wherever God's people are sharing the words of the Bible in gift and in deed."

NETTIE (WILSON) HOFFMAN

1950 - 51

I spent two summers (1950 and 1951) at Golden Prairie. The first summer I was not studying theology. I must confess I had no idea about the development of worship service. I recall asking Mrs. May how we begin the service. She said, "We generally sing the Doxology." I said: "What's that?"

You see, I was a student in the School of Law at the University of Toronto. I had been with the Royal Canadian Mounted Police stationed in various parts of Saskatchewan: Rose Valley, Regina, and Melville. During the war I served with the Royal Canadian Navy. After the war I went to the University of Toronto to study Law and prepare myself to return to the RCM Police as an officer. However, I was not entirely content with that goal although I enjoyed my experience with the police. So I applied to the United Church for a mission placement and I came to Golden Prairie to find my way.

It was at Golden Prairie that I made my decision to become an ordained minister. I was not even a member of the United Church at that time. I think I became a candidate for the ministry at Maple Creek. At any rate, Golden Prairie offered me a wonderful opportunity to discover what I wanted to do with my life.

I can assure you that I was not much of a Minister and the sermons must have been nothing short of horrendous. However, prairie people are long suffering. They were so warm and loving and supportive. I remember arriving there feeling entirely lost, confused, and uncertain whether I should be there. In fact, I was quite certain that I had made a very big mistake. I sat in the little manse wondering what I should do. Then I heard a soft rap at the door. It was little Albert Henderson bearing a gift from his mother – a hot apple pie. What a great welcome!

What started in Golden Prairie opened the way to a remarkable journey with pastorates in northern Ontario, Quebec, Rhode Island, USA, Manchester, England, southern Ontario, Toronto, and finally to a University chaplaincy and a teaching appointment at the University. During that journey I completed a doctoral degree in psychology and clinical studies.

I am stimulated once again to make a sentimental journey to Golden Prairie. I wonder if anyone would know me there? I am sure I would find a warm welcome … prairie people are like that. Writing this fills me with warm feelings and happy memories.

ALVIN L. EVANS

1 9 5 2

The church at Golden Prairie was important to me also, though I was there for such a short time, and so many years ago. The year that Nettie Wilson served there I met her at Camp Shagabec, and was greatly influenced by her in my decision to prepare for work in the ministry in the church. It was a surprise and overwhelming challenge to find myself in Golden Prairie just three summers later, trying to continue the work that she and Al Evans had been doing. I must confess that my own talents seemed very limited in comparison to theirs.

I do remember, with affection, some very special families and young people – Paul and Rose Martin, Pearl and Leonard Arnold were especially helpful and supportive, as was George Murray. It is thirty-six years since then, and I have forgotten many names, and much of the detail, but I will try to recall just a few things that will reflect the experience.

Coming to Golden Prairie was, for me, easier than for some students. It was almost like coming home, for I grew up on a prairie farm not far away. I knew prairie people, and to some extent understood their personalities, their hopes and fears, their problems, their friendships. Coming as the "student minister" was more difficult, though I approached that with more self-confidence and assurance than I would have years later when I had learned how little I really knew! I did leave feeling humbled by the experience, and more questioning of the way that I should serve the church.

How would I describe my summer? I was met by gracious, friendly people, who were ready to help me in every way. I very much appreciated that. I was challenged by thoughtful people who made me really think about what was unique about Christianity. I remember with affection the young people who were active in the Sunday School, attended Vacation School, and sang in the girls' choir. I learned the importance of disciplined study and action even though it was often difficult. Sermon preparation, regular visitation, planning for classes, all affect how well we are able to bring the gospel message.

My supervising pastor in Maple Creek, the Reverend Alf Day, was a great inspiration and help. He listened to my problems and ideas, and offered valuable, practical help. When I arrived in Golden Prairie, I was presented with a light motor bike that was to have been my summer transportation. I was not able to start it myself and I think made one bumpy windy journey on it to a nearby farm. Somewhere I got a bicycle for replacement, but found trips to Burstall better completed by riding the mail truck, and getting rides from local people. Mr. Day convinced a number of men to give $10 to $25 each to the purchase of a second-hand Ford, and helped me practise for my driving test which I passed on the second try. That made travelling much easier, and aside from one flat tire and one descent from the high road to the ditch, all went reasonably well.

There were some problems. Several times I found a man's footprints under my bedroom window, and that caused me some worry and concern. I learned to draw the curtains very tight. One of the the local "town drunks" came to my doorstep late one night wanting to talk. I spent a while with him outside before he went home, and in the morning called his daughter to pick up the case of beer that he had left behind. I managed to alienate some people I had expected to be communicants that summer, and that was upsetting. I frequently heard about how wonderful the previous student had been, and though I knew it was true, it was often discouraging.

On the whole, it was a positive experience, and I thank the churches in the little prairie towns for the help they have given to all of us as we sought to learn and grow in our faith so that we might better serve the Lord. I did not go on to ordination. I met and married the Rev. Doug Crichton. We served together, nine years at Wynyard and Outlook before moving to New

Jersey where he did graduate work. Doug has taught since 1968 at Queen's Theological College, and I have continued to do a number of small things in the church: Sunday School, study groups, and visitation. I have worked, sometimes full-time and sometimes part-time, as a teacher and a library assistant. We have four grown children and three grandchildren. It has been my dream for the past few years to finish the studies I began in 1949. Whether I ever do or not, I will remember the summer at Golden Prairie as a positive step on my journey of faith and I will remember the people with love and affection.

VIOLET CRICHTON

1954 - 55

My first experience as a Student Minister was at Golden Prairie, Saskatchewan. Looking back over the two summers spent there I realize how much those fine people gave in the way of love and understanding – far more, I'm afraid, than I gave in return.

I can still recall the loneliness felt when stepping off the train at Maple Creek at two o'clock in the morning. I was totally alone, on the station platform, in complete darkness. I wondered at the time how I ever got into that situation. However, my fears were soon put to rest when my supervising pastor came to the station. He was the Rev. Alfred Day of Maple Creek. He became a fine friend as well as a great source of information and inspiration.

What the little one-room Manse lacked in creature comforts was soon compensated for by the friendliness of the townsfolk. In spite of all the meals, that were so graciously provided by so many kind people, by the end of the summer I counted the Massong's grocery slips and discovered that I had devoured seventy-eight cans of pork and beans. By the end of the summer I didn't even bother heating them. That says something about my cooking abilities.

During the first summer Bill Zeliznik, the Station Master, and I borrowed a tractor and a grader and with a lot of help we built a tennis court. This proved to be a fine attraction for many young people. I'm afraid my tennis playing was on par with my cooking.

I remember becoming a supply teacher in the High School, when one of the teachers became ill. I really didn't know much about teaching, but the class was very patient and kind. They taught me more than I taught them.

I learned to drive a car during my first summer, under the patient teaching of George Murray. Shortly after I arrived at the Manse, Len Arnold and Paul Martin brought me the student minister's car, a 1934 Chevrolet. It proved to be a great car. I'd give my eye teeth to own it now. When I informed them that I couldn't drive they said that I had better learn because I had a church service in Richmound, some twenty miles north, the following Sunday. Somehow I managed, and drove most of the summer without a license. Before the summer was over I bought my first car, a 1949 Chevrolet. It was a fine car. It even had automatic directional lights which were illegal in Saskatchewan. The following summer I traded the car in for a 1948 Chrysler–one of the finest cars I've owned.

I used to enjoy helping the farmers with their harvesting. It was great fun driving the tractors. The second summer I actually worked for three weeks for an old gentleman, Mr. Suttaby, who could not find labourers to help him. He had an old 1928 tractor which worked like a charm.

The names that will forever remain in my memory are of the people who were exceptionally kind to me and who treated me like a member of their family. These were: Paul and Rose Martin; Len and Pearl Arnold; Helen and Jack Campbell; George Murray; the Gardiners; the Swaoks; and the Schlahts. There were many others, of course, but time has unkindly erased their names from my memory.

I feel I was greatly privileged and most fortunate to have spent two summers among the good people of the Golden Prairie area. My only feeling of remorse comes when I realize how terribly inadequate was my ministry there. But the kind folks gave of their love in spite of all my failings. "Blest be the tie that binds."

JIM MACINTOSH

1958-59

I have often reflected on the idea that those of us who have served what we used to call "Student Fields" have been privileged and fortunate persons. It is a rather unique opportunity and experience. Comparatively speaking, very few people can do this. At the time I was a student in both Arts and Theology, I was conscious of the fact that I could have a fascinating lifestyle. For approximately half the year, I walked the corridors of "academia," and climbed "ivory towers." For the other half of the year, the Church provided us with the opportunity to travel, meet people, live in places which we would not ordinarily otherwise know, and engage in work which we hope is not only useful in itself, but valuable as practical preparation for one's life's work.

Canada is an amazingly vast and diverse land. As a Student Minister, I had the opportunity to experience both of these qualities first-hand. I have never regretted the fact that each summer during each college year, I took advantage of this marvellous system which the United Church has developed to serve on Mission Fields. This gave me an opportunity to serve such geographically and culturally diverse areas as Hines Creek in the Peace River country of Alberta, where homesteading, even in the '50s, was not a thing of the past, and where immigrants from the Ukraine, especially among the women, spoke little or no English and clung to many of their cherished traditions from the old country. Mission fields in the Maritimes – Nova Scotia, in the community of Vaughans and New Brunswick, Southfield, Harcourt – gave an opportunity to experience rural life, and the Church life of smaller congregations, which I had not experienced before, having been brought up in the city and in a large congregation.

One of these Maritime fields was an extremely fortunate experience for at least one person – perhaps two! – inasmuch as I met Marilyn, my wife, there, although she was from the larger nearby city of Moncton. She has insisted on moving with me to every Pastoral Charge since then!

And then Golden Prairie!! I had such a fine time my first summer in Golden Prairie that I insisted the Church send me back there for a second summer. At that time, it was generally against the regulations, but I really felt I deserved a second chance, and that I might be able to repair some of the damage done during the first summer! They bought it! Life had been so pleasant under the hot prairie sun, with an equal brightness and warmth from the fine Prairie people, that I really felt it was a rare privilege to be able to return for a second summer. It was great to have the feeling that one was returning, rather than coming for the first time. It was great to see scenes and people that one had become familiar with, and at home amongst, because even the experience of going on a Mission Field for the first time entails certain understandable emotions.

The posting of appointments in the spring amongst students at a theological college was anxiously awaited with a mixture of dread and enthusiasm, for the voice of Church authorities was in many respects like the voice of God – not to be argued with, and one which determined our future. A good question to be debated in bull sessions at that time of year amongst theologues was, "Was it indeed Divine Providence, predestination, or blind fate which was responsible for the casting of our lots?" "You go here," or "you go there." So often it was, and perhaps still is, necessary for us to leave our future fate in the hands of those whom we hope and pray are wise enough to make the right decision for both the young, aspiring pastor, and the faithful, hopeful (and sometimes long-suffering) people.

Golden Prairie was a happy choice made on my behalf, from my point of view, from the word "go". From the first time the word tingled off the appointment letter, Golden Prairie had a romantic sound to it. Even its geographical location was ideal, smack in the middle of the real prairies. The reality lived up to the promise of the name, and the expectations that the promise gave birth to: not just a typical prairie town, but indeed the perfect example of a prairie town – just large enough, and just small enough, with the right number of wheat elevators like ornaments along the necklace of the railway track; not skimpy, with just one or two elevators, like prairie towns that were almost excuses for towns, nor too large like some that were overgrown and really didn't deserve the snug fitting title "town" any more; flat as a pancake, with magnificent sunrises and sunsets. I actually did see a few sunrises, but many more sunsets! One of the perks of being a Student Minister was that one did not really have to rise early. There were no early calls – no phone! I learned easily – it was second nature to me – to take advantage of all the perks. The long, straight highways, with few turns, so unlike the typical traditional winding roads of the east; and the wheat fields stretching out in all directions all around the town.

   I used to boast that I was probably the only Student Minister in Canada with two cars. Golden Prairie was unique in that sense. Some years before my arrival on the scene, a benefactor in Maple Creek had willed his car to the Church – Maple Creek Church, that is. Memory fails one in so many details. I would love to be able to remember the year and make of the old car which I drove for so many miles. Its vintage would be somewhere in the '30s, but it was a comfortable and reliable old companion, and as I recall, gave little or no problem. It was a pretty shade of light green, and would now be quite a classic to own. An arrangement had been struck with the Golden Prairie folk that the student would have the use of the car in exchange for conducting services in Maple Creek during the Minister's vacation. So for both years I was there, during Mel Ryan's vacation, I conducted a 9:30 am service in the lovely modern Maple Creek Church. I would drive to Maple Creek on Saturday evening, be billeted with one of the Church families, conduct my first service, then drive to Golden Prairie for the 11:00 am service there. Besides the Church car, I had a '51 Pontiac which I had driven from Nova Scotia to Saskatchewan, and which, of course, I drove back to Nova Scotia each year. During the summer, I would, of course, use their car. So I was the only student to have two vehicles. The only drawback with the Maple Creek car, as I recall, was that the gas gauge did not work. This had a tendency to make one nervous as I was often not quite sure how much gas was left in the tank!

It was during my second summer in Golden Prairie that the Church interior was renovated. The arrangement had been that of a central pulpit, with the choir seated on back, facing the congregation. With a good deal of volunteer work, and with many items of memorial furniture, the chancel area was made into a divided chancel, with the pulpit on the side and the lectern on the other, the Communion Table in the center, and the choir loft divided as well.

I have a good number of slides of the two summers in Golden Prairie. Some of those pictures are of the choir. I was very proud of the choir, and as regularly as we could, we would have choir practice. It was, of course, difficult to gather people together during summer evenings on a regular basis for this. The slides show the choir members proudly decked out in their black gowns. We can't tell by looking at them, but they are really Nova Scotia gowns. My home Church, St. Andrew's, Halifax, had acquired new gowns, and appropriately enough, the gowns that had been replaced found their way to Golden Prairie. It may be my imagination, but I always felt the choir sang better in their newly-acquired gowns! Certainly they (both choir and gowns) added to the dignity of the service.

One of the lovely aspects of being a single student on a Mission Field was the way in which many of the families took the student "under their wing," especially in the area of providing a meal. This guaranteed that, despite their own occasional self-prepared and self-inflicted meal, the student had sufficient nutrition and delicious meals, so there is little danger of losing any weight during the summer. An invitation to a meal is more than merely an invitation to eat. There is the friendship and comaraderie which goes along with a meal. I had so many free meals at the Martins that I almost, but not quite, began to feel guilty as a free-loader! Also, I ate at such homes at the Pohls and Gardiners, as well as a host of others.

I can remember the surprise and jealousy with which fellow student ministers greeted my boast that on the Golden Prairie charge, I had only one service a Sunday to conduct. Many of the other students had three.

I have tried to emphasize the sense of adventure and the sense of privilege which were part of the experience of being a student minister in Golden Prairie. But, of course, the important thing to emphasize is the people one met. They opened their hearts and homes to student after student, summer after summer. It must be quite a different experience to be part of a church community served by summer student ministers than that of a church served by a full-time ordained minister. Student fields have to have special people in them. Students were, in my day, mostly single men. Most of them came from the East, and would be far from family and friends. Parishioners on the student field had to be supportive and caring in a special way. They also had to be very understanding, as by the nature of the situation, student ministers were learners and experimenters. This is surely why most ministers who have served student fields have a very soft spot in their hearts for their particular fields and their individual experiences. They never forget the fine folk who were so welcoming and sharing. Student fields can make or break a student by either confirming his or her compatibility with Ministry, or they can be disillusioning experiences whereby one could find one's "calling" questioned. How can one measure the debt one owes to the wonderful persons who nurtured and fed them – in more ways than one?

    I have often imagined how nice it would be to be able to re-visit, after such a comparatively long lapse of time, to see the inevitable changes, but also the inevitable sameness of the community. I would imagine that many of the same names are still to be found. I remember such names as Murray, Beach, Stern, Roth, Krahn, Widmer, Swaok, Luker, as well as Martin, Pohl, Broome, and Gardiner.

    Well do I remember arriving in Golden Prairie in the early spring of 1959 for my second year to find snow on the ground and a chill in the air. The one-room manse was set in a lovely secluded spot, next to the Church, with lilac bushes in the front yard and a path to the not-so-modern "convenience" in an auxiliary hut about 4 x 4 in the back! I remember the Manse as being about 20 x 30 feet. The furnishings consisted of a wood stove, kitchen table, a smaller table which served as a desk, a small set of book shelves on the wall, one bed, and two or three chairs.

As I scanned through my slides of those years, I saw pictures of the ladies of the Church performing the "bucket and mop brigade," and the "paint brigade." The church basement had suffered some water damage some time before my arrival the first year, and with great enthusiasm, the ladies set to work to not only clean up the damage, but to patch and paint, so that the end result was a beautiful, bright and useful basement hall. Other slides show the same type of enthusiastic work being carried out on the Manse with, for example, Mrs. Gardiner, who was at least well into her 70s at that time, swinging a paint brush with apparent relish and expertise.

Scenes of vacation school concerts, Confirmation classes, and Baptismal services are the subjects of other slides. One wonders where some of the young people are now as adults, but who still smile youthfully and coyly from the screen, like Keats' "Ode on a Grecian Urn": "Eternally caught in their youth." Behind the pictures are many stories.

How appropriate that the Treasurer of the Church, Mr. Murray, should have been a genuine Scot right from the old country, who had farmed near Golden Prairie for many years, but during my time there was retired and lived on the street behind the Manse and Church.

One of the difficulties in keeping in contact, or not seeing people, is the tremendous size of Canada. We are so far away. It was an absolute delight some years after those student days in Golden Prairie to have two families (in different years) visit us in New Brunswick – the Pohls and the Martins. Their visits were all too short, but it was great to be able to talk about Golden Prairie and its people. The Martins were rather impressed with a grandfather clock which we had in the Manse, and which had been made by the Loyalist Clock Company in Sheffield, New Brunswick, which was just across the Saint John River from where we were living in Oromocto. So impressed were they that they visited the Loyalist Clock people and arranged to have a similar grandfather clock shipped all the way to Golden Prairie. They now live, of course, in Medicine Hat. We hear from Paul and Rose every Christmas, and Paul assures us that the Loyalist grandfather clock is still ticking away accurately and faithfully, and it can't help but remind them of their trip to the east, and their visit with the Kings.

Such reminiscences of necessity must be random and partial. There is so much one would like to reminisce about. Reminiscences come and go over the years. Sometimes one is reminded of a person or an incident because of a present experience. How true Browning's insight is when he said, "I am a part of all that I have met."

To sum it all up, I have a warm and bright glow when I recall the days and experiences of Golden Prairie. One story can illustrate the sense of acceptance and accomplishment I received from the responsive people there. From a student minister's point of view, the annual Confirmation class would have been quite a challenge and very important. Both years we had large and enthusiastic Confirmation classes, which met in the little Manse, some people sitting on the bed even, and we probably had to bring in chairs from the Church next door.

The morning that I left Golden Prairie for the last time, I went to get in my '51 Pontiac, and found a note attached to the steering wheel. It was a note of appreciation from a

Vacation School, August 1958

young married couple, both of whom had attended Confirmation classes. They may still be living in Golden Prairie and recognize themselves in this story. Their note expressed appreciation for the fact that Confirmation classes had given them a new perspective on the Church. Their attitude had been a mixture between embarrassment and indifference, together with elements of questioning and uncertainty regarding their Christian heritage. Our times together had clarified many fuzzy points for them, and had given them a new confidence so that they were now much happier and more secure in their faith and Churchmanship. Needless to say, such a testimony was very much appreciated on my part, and served as a welcome going away present.

HAROLD KING

1960

During the spring of 1960 I was completing a BA at the University of Saskatchewan and living in residence at St. Andrew's College. Having worked the previous three summers at a bakery in Regina, I was looking for a different experience before embarking on my final year as an undergraduate student. My plans were to go into Education and become a high school teacher. Little did I realize that the summer ahead would turn out to be one of the most memorable of my life.

The idea of serving on a rural mission field was fairly familiar to me because of my contact with Theology students who did this on a regular basis. Although I was aware that occasionally the United Church would place students who had not committed themselves to going into the ministry, I did not really expect that my application for a student mission field would be accepted.

It was therefore with considerable surprise and not a little trepidation that I opened the letter informing me that I would spending the summer at the one-point charge of Golden Prairie, Saskatchewan. Golden Prairie – the name evoked images of lush ripening grain fields. Its location on a hastily found map of the province, however, suggested otherwise, since it was discovered to be in a part of the province better suited to ranching than abundant wheat crops.

Having survived the initial shock of realizing what the summer would hold, I made plans for the move and began contemplating the almost five months of church services and sermons for which I would be responsible.

In thinking about the summer spent in Golden Prairie, one recalls it initially in personal terms. There is no doubt that the experience was a remarkable one in so many ways, particularly in the personal relationships which were developed and the friendships that exist to this day. It's easy to recall the people who made the summer in Golden Prairie so special, as well as some of the events which characterized those few months. But to try to assess the contribution one might have made to the spiritual life of the community or the development of the church is more difficult.

Appearance-wise, the church looked as attractive in 1960 as it would probably ever look. The renovations which had been initiated the previous year were completed that summer, thanks to Alec Broome and the men of the congregation. I was convinced the United Church in Golden Prairie was as lovely as any rural church in the province, and would take great pride in showing pictures of it.

What about other signs of vitality? Church attendance, I believe, was up that year, as were contributions, although our donations to the St. Andrew's extension fund were fairly modest. A small but successful Vacation School was held, along with Sunday School and Explorers. Special Sundays included Mother's Day, Anniversary Sunday and the service at which Communion was served and new members joined the church by baptism and profession of faith. This service was conducted by Rev. Watkinson, who had recently arrived to become the Maple Creek minister.

The only people to form a communicant's class were the Babitzky's, a family with two teenage boys who farmed near Richmound. It was easy to schedule classes, as they would be held at their farm, usually in conjunction with a large meal. Eating out was one of the delights (and weight-wise, the hazards) of the summer, especially when one has a fondness for fried chicken.

I suppose one of the shortcomings of my ministry related to the amount of visiting which I did. While I could use as an excuse the fact that I wasn't accustomed to ministers who dropped in unannounced, or didn't have the car until into July, or liked to spend time more with some people than with others, I should have been more diligent in visiting every family in the congregation.

One can always rationalize that it's the quality rather than the quantity of time one spends visiting, and I would like to believe that people enjoyed having me as a guest. Other than asking the blessing at meals, I don't believe God entered the conversations regularly. As with most student ministers, I was relieved that no funerals had to be conducted during the summer. The week at Camp Shagabec could hardly be considered a highly religious experience.

I have learned over the years that if one contributes to the best of one's ability, the rewards are typically far greater than one expects or deserves. That was certainly true during the summer I spent in Golden Prairie. While I would like to believe that I gave of my best, I received so much more in return. The sentiments I expressed at the last service are all the more true to this day.

Occasions and People Recalled:
- visits to the Sulz's, George Murray and the Dunwald's
- having fresh buns with tuna filling with Connie Swaok and occasionally Lena May in Connie's tiny kitchen.
- golfing occasionally with Jerome Martin and Bruce Schau (and actually beating them, that is when we could find the balls in the tall grass)
- the "monster" dance at Fox Valley
- the visit from close friends in Saskatoon who came down for one weekend
- sitting in the basement of the Baptist Church for the funeral service of one of the prominent women in the community
- visiting Cathy Martin in the hospital in Maple Creek when she had her appendix removed
- sharing my limited grocery purchases with the two stores in town
- driving into Maple Creek in Eddie Pohl's new 1959 Mercury for the induction of Rev. Watkinson (Lydia making sure I watched where I was going)
- advising Connie that since it was an evening service she didn't need to wear a hat, and then discovering she was the only one without one
- discovering that the people who had the farthest to come were usually the first to get to church on Sunday
- meeting Olga Sawby, Inez Swaok and (the lovely) Shirley Stern
- preaching during August at Maple Creek (the first Sunday the Watkinson children slept in and missed my best sermon)
- trips to "the Hat," the Park and to Saskatoon with the Martins
- enjoying fresh bread and peanut butter in the Martins' kitchen
- getting used to hair curlers and people asking in cafes how fresh the pie was.

TERRY MCKAGUE

1 9 6 5

One of the first greetings I received when I arrived in Golden Prairie in May of 1965 was, "Welcome to the West." I guess people were used to giving this greeting because most of the student ministers who came to the United Church in Golden Prairie came from "The East". I was an exception to this, coming from Edmonton, so I wasn't introduced to the West, but I was certainly welcomed into that small but dedicated community of people who every spring would awaken Golden Prairie United Church from its winter's slumber and bring it to life again.

In this book Jerome Martin describes a debt he feels to the many student ministers who came to serve on the Golden Prairie pastoral charge. Thinking back on my summer there, I realize that it was a time of learning and growing for me far more than for the members of the church. It could be fairly said that many ministers in the United Church of Canada, and also the congregations they have gone on to serve, are indebted to Golden Prairie, and other communities like it, for the patient love with which they have helped so many aspiring ministers along the way to fulfilling their calling.

The summer I was appointed to the Golden Prairie pastoral charge I was also asked to take occasional services in Burstall, Saskatchewan, a town several miles north of Golden Prairie and slightly west, almost on the Alberta border. It was in travelling north of Golden Prairie, on a road that seemed to go in a straight line forever, that I discovered by first-hand experience exactly how far it is between "Correction Lines." Then coming back south one rainy night I discovered that if you put your car into a hundred and eighty degree spin you can break the seals on two tires at once, leaving you with two flats and only one spare. I was on Highway 21 south of Fox Valley at the time and managed to hitch hike my way south to Martins' farm where, of course, I was in good hands.

My appointment to Burstall was in some ways a strange one. There was no existing United Church congregation or building, but the community was growing because of a natural gas processing plant attached to the Trans-Canada Pipeline and the United Church seemed anxious to establish a presence there. The anomaly in the situation was that there was an Evangelical United Brethren Church in Burstall and within a few short years that denomination had joined with the United Church of Canada.

During my summer in Golden Prairie I was fortunate to have the supervision of the Reverend Boyd Beckle of the United Church in Maple Creek. What was particularly enriching in working with him was the opportunity to see him carry forward his ministry while suffering severely from the effects of Parkinson's Disease.

Burstall may have been growing at that time because of the proximity of the pipe line, but most small prairie towns were not. My recollection is that there was an underlying fear amongst the people of Golden Prairie, as in many small communities, that the consolidation of services, which had already doomed so many small centres, could advance further and threaten the life of relatively viable communities like Golden Prairie. It seemed a very peculiar thing that prairie towns could be born and grow and then decline and die all within forty or fifty years. As I recall, the people of Golden Prairie lived with some fear that the small and relatively new rail spur which terminated three was in peril of being abandoned.

I did not proceed in a straight line towards ordained ministry after my summer in Golden Prairie. But having pursued some other interests and studies for a few years, I returned to training for the ministry at the Vancouver School of Theology in 1978, by which time I was married to my wife Jane and we had two small children. I was ordained by Alberta Conference in 1981 and transferred to the Montreal and Ottawa Conference at my request. Here in Quebec I have served a three-point charge in the Laurentian Mountains north of Montreal for five years and am now in my fourth year serving a suburban congregation on the island of Montreal. We now have five children ranging in age from thirteen to two.

I have never been back to Golden Prairie since the summer of 1965, so in my memory the people and places have been frozen as they were then. I am anxious, when this book comes out, to read more about the community that was my home for a very brief but a very significant part of my life.

FRANK GIFFEN

1 9 6 6

To actually be in ministry with real people, real issues, and real spiritual needs was a profound experience. It made my call to ministry very real and human, rather than just a possibility in theory. I remember planning worship details, music, vacation school, and home and hospital visits. Meals out were wonderful, and in this hospitality I sensed a genuine caring that was the strength of the church.

In 1966 I was on my second summer field, aged 20, and had just finished my BA degree from McMaster in Hamilton. I remember that summer as a time of my life when I both knew a lot and knew very little. I was often confronted with each of these realities. Talking with the old men who sat on wooden benches along the sidewalk in Golden Prairie was both fascinating and enlightening. From them I learned about crop yields, the dirty thirties, and the pride they had in the land and in the west. They told me the early stories of how the land had been opened up and the difficulties and joys of early days. This was all fresh and alive to me, a young city boy who knew little of the events they described.

The surrounding country was beautiful. I remember the height of the grain, the rolling hills, the gumbo, and the sunsets. All of this was new and awe-inspiring.

The visit from Armand Stade, the district superintendent, was welcomed. He was the only "supervision" of any kind that happened for me that summer. My named supervisor in Maple Creek was very ill and almost not functioning that summer. Therefore, I was very much on my own. Armand and I talked about how I was doing ministry, and he was supportive and informative. The most distressing part of the visit was that his wife had travelled with him, and sat in the car for the hour he talked with me! I invited her in, but they had agreed that she would wait for him to finish his visit.

I drove a red Volkswagen "bug" that year, and was surprised and delighted to find a VW dealership right in town! When I would pull up for gas, local people would tease me about only needing a few drops for my car. I was pulled out of the mud one day by a tractor. We put the chains on the wrong place, and I twisted the "handles" on the back bumper. Soon, a new set arrived and the repair was quickly made right at home.

Living in the little house beside the church was practical and fun for a single man. The little path to the outhouse wasn't new for me, but took an adjustment to live this way for a whole summer. I remember walking up to Pohl's each week for my bath! Mr. Pohl loved to eat raw hot peppers as a snack and we would share them together after my bath!

I will never forget my first experience of hail. The pounding on the metal roof was dramatic. I was amazed at how high the hailstones bounced off the sidewalk. I was distressed to see flattened crops, and felt very helpless in the face of the destruction.

The Martin family was most hospitable. I remember fondly our trips to the "Hat". As a city boy, it felt good to be once again among tall buildings and a great variety of stores and services.

The rural experience had great charm, and was a very significant ministry for me. When I was back in theological school, the people and issues of Golden Prairie were very fresh and alive for me. They provided a reality test for all the theory and theology we were dealing with. Those experiences encouraged me to continue in training for the ministry, and were foundational for much that has happened since.

KEITH E. W. GROSS

1969

Golden Prairie was my first church mission field. I had never been that far away from home on my own before. When I arrived, I was warmly greeted by Rev. Rod & Marion Francis. When I arrived at Golden Prairie, Rose and Paul Martin took me under their wings, for which I was always grateful.

I have no bad memories of my summer in Golden Prairie. The western hospitality was in full bloom as far as I was concerned. People were very receptive to my incompetence, to my interests, to my lifestyle. The names escape me, but I remember with fondness an elderly couple (in their 80s) who would feed me soup for lunch and mold me into a Saskatchewan Roughrider fan. It was Golden Prairie that made me a Canadian football league

Pew and book rack, Golden Prairie United Church

supporter and to this day, the Roughriders team is my team. I was so pleased to see them when they came East a number of years ago. The people were all very supportive and certainly allowed me and others to be themselves. This experience gave me a good start in faith development and in seeing people in the capacity of being basically supportive.

The only problem I had was getting used to an outside toilet and having no television to watch. The open homes more than made up for that. I was probably best known as the student with the red Volkswagon. I had fun with that car. I took it to the Rockies; I drove it in the most unlikely places. One day I rolled it at Bald Butte in the Cypress Hills, and had to drive it to Maple Creek with no windows and with the doors tied shut. The chap who sold me the car and who was always there to help me, took the car and sawed the roof off. For the next 5 or 6 weeks, I drove it as a convertible and it only rained once in that period of time!

LARRY HARRISON

1 9 7 0

I have very fond memories of my Golden Prairie days as it was my first experience of practical ministry and of western Canada. It became the beginning of a love affair with the United Church and the people of Saskatchewan. I'm not sure that means I think that Saskatchewan is the best part of Canada, but it has become my home.

I travelled west on the train from Mount Allison University to Swift Current (a train trip no longer possible) and then on to Maple Creek by bus. After a day or two with the Francis family in Maple Creek, I headed north to Golden Prairie in my old pelter of a car. I thought I was fairly well prepared to face this rural, western experience, having had the opportunity to talk to Larry Harrison before leaving the east. But after arriving at the manse, there certainly was an overshadowing sense of loneliness in this wide open prairie. There were to be many firsts for me that summer.

Fortunately, it didn't take me too long to find the families and individuals who would be the "church family" and my main supporters. One vivid memory of mine is the alkaline water from the well pump on the other side of the church. I had been "warned and instructed" to some degree about its "qualities," but one evening I tried to shampoo my hair in a basin full of this heinous liquid only to ruefully discover it made a mess of my hair, causing it to become like straw or half-cooked spaghetti. Nothing I could do would normalize my hair. What a sight I must have been! And what a sense of panic soon seized my soul! To my rescue came Connie Swaok and Lena May. They had come along to check on me and discovered my predicament. To their credit, neither laughed in front of me and Connie left right away to bring me a pail of rain water to rinse my hair in. What a relief! After that I took much more seriously Paul and Rose Martin's offer of their home for my "bath house."

I also have memories of getting stuck in that rain-soaked western mud (they don't teach us how to drive in that stuff back east), of my first Vacation Church School, of riding in a harvest combine for the first time, of visits to the Cypress Hills, and of the western sunsets (during which on Saturdays I was usually writing sermons). There are certainly the memories of the people who had to put up with yet another greenhorn student minister: the Dave Gardiners, George Murray, Cliff and Dorothy Dunwald, as well as the aforementioned Martins, Swaoks Mays, and others. I fear to think what my sermons must have been like, or my visiting style; but I have no reservation in expressing thanks for the folks who made such a strong impression on me and introduced me to the province I would come to feel so much at home in.

BILL CORKEM

1 9 7 1

I admit I do not have a great many specific memories of my summer at Golden Prairie. But, in many ways, it was the summer I grew up. Looking back, I marvel at how the good people there survived at all.

1971 was the first time I had been so far from my home on Prince Edward Island, so I had to deal with a bit of homesickness. This is where Paul and Rose Martin were of such unbelievable help to me.

I certainly remember the little house in Golden Prairie. I could fit the house into my present living room. And running water meant running next door for it. And out behind the house stood the formidable outhouse.

I also remember the first funeral at which I officiated. And the Sunday following Mrs. Gardiner's funeral I decided to change one of the hymns since we had sung that particular one at her funeral. My choice was still not good for my particular selection (I can't remember which it was) had most of the congregation in tears. And singing is not my strong point!

That summer I gained a better understanding of westerners and their way of life. Their warmth and faith are unsurpassed anywhere.

What I learned and gained in 1971 continues with me and is a part of my ministry today. Primarily, it was the ministry of the people rather than just my ministry.

ELAINE PALMER

1 9 7 3

It was on May 1, 1973, that I arrived in Golden Prairie, Saskatchewan. At the tender age of nineteen, my trip to Golden Prairie marked the first occasion in which I spent any extended period away from my home.

This adventure was both frightening and exciting. After I overcame some initial homesickness, I settled in experiencing the generous hospitality of the community and of my supervisor, the Rev. Rodney Francis. As I look back upon my experience I believe that I displayed all the signs of an immature teenager. Although there was some growth in my faith and my practice of ministry, Golden Prairie really provided me with an opportunity to "grow up." Interestingly, it tended to be the non-church folk who made a particular effort to befriend me. I became acquainted with a farmer named Lavern, and a teacher named Larry, who introduced me to such things as grooming horses, throwing bales, and some prairie night life.

I will forever remain indebted to Braydon Hirsch, who, although barely a teenager himself, became a host to me and I believe many other student ministers. Braydon was there to support and befriend me and regrettably I have lost touch with him over the years.

Due to the efforts of Rodney Francis, I worked at improving my worship leadership, encountered my first funeral service, organized my first vacation school, and began to do some self-service. In retrospect I would have to state that Golden Prairie was an incomparable experience in which I began to move from teenager to young adulthood. This developmental stage in my life combined with the hospitality and acceptance of the people of Golden Prairie, made it a summer that I will always remember.

Brian Walton

1 9 7 4

My summer at Golden Prairie influenced my attitudes: about the prairies, about small towns, about farming, about ministry, and about myself. I had driven through Saskatchewan only by train before that summer. I was overwhelmed with the sunsets and sunrises, the horizon so long and open. The fresh air was refreshing compared to my home base, Toronto.

I grew to admire the hard-working farmers in the area, including my next door neighbours, the Hirsch family. My experiential education in farming was in loading and stacking bales for the Paul Martins and one other family. I felt that experience the next day.

Arnie Chamberlain and a friend

I enjoyed the closeness of the one-room manse to the church, the nearby Post Office and the grocery store. Everyone knew everyone, which made the summer stimulating.

Some highlights of my sumer at Golden Prairie were: getting my driver's license on the second try, Vacation Bible School, Cypress Hills camp, and the many visits with Golden Prairie people.

One learning experience for me happened one Saturday evening. I was both energetic and naive in church matters. I had a brilliant idea: I thought that Christian worship was a time when people should see each other, rather than the backs of heads. I (wisely) turned all of the pews sideways, still having the aisle in the centre. I was practising my theology. Wow! How exciting! A short time later one member of the congregation came to talk with me. Oops! I had not asked anyone about changing the pews! In approximately three seconds the pews were in their original positions. What a lesson! I now see this experience as one of the most humorous of my summer in Golden Prairie.

Two difficulties of my summer were: being single and finding out where some families lived on the sideroads.

All in all, I came to love the prairies and the people who lived there. The proof of this is in that I married Rita Cattell from Regina. We have been married ten years and have two children: Ryan (4 years) and Michael (15 months). Calgary, Alberta is now our home. I remember most of the people from Golden Prairie. Jenny Glennie and Connie Swaok I visited often, and Olive Blohm gave me a camping-sunset painting I still treasure. My summer at Golden Prairie was challenging and fun. My memories are deep and precious. God's presence was very real in Golden Prairie. I praise God that I've been a part of its history and life.

ARNIE CHAMBERLAIN